CONTENTS

I0440161

WHY DO YOU NEED AI?

Dmitrii Mergus | Dinesh Kumar

Introducing **AI Marketing Engineers**, your
Revenue Optimization Experts Dinesh and Dmitrii.

Why Choose Us?

- **Proven Track Record of Success:** We have generated over **$1 Billion in sales**, showcasing our deep industry expertise.
- **ROI-Focused:** Every prompt, insight, and resource is designed to ensure substantial returns on your investment.

Unlock Marketing Creativity with "AI Marketing Guide"

In this book, you'll:

- **Navigate Through AI:** Explore handpicked marketing prompts crafted by seasoned experts.
- **Practical Guide:** From best practices to prompt engineering, discover how to generate images, enhance your skills, and more.
- **Boost Efficiency:** Elevate your productivity with AI.
- Innovate Swiftly: Quickly develop and deploy cutting-edge marketing ideas that work.

Join us at the forefront of the marketing revolution. For insights, support, and a suite of resources designed to skyrocket your marketing into a new era, connect with us at aimarketingengineers.com.

THE AI REVENUE ARCHITECT

Dinesh Kumar Chinnasamy

Seattle, WA

- Position: VP of Analytics & Paid Customer Acquisition
- Experience: 15+ years
- Education: MBA, B.Sc. in Computer Science

750 Million+ in revenue through bridging Data and Innovation:
Transforming Marketing with AI Expertise

- **Tech Roots to Marketing Magnate:** Started in software engineering, honing a strong technical foundation. Transitioned to an Analytics-Powered Marketing Strategist, focusing on data-driven strategies to enhance customer engagement and drive sustainable business growth.
- **AI and Marketing Innovator:** Distinguished in utilizing AI, Deep Learning, and Reinforcement Learning, transforming marketing strategies with technological finesse. His expertise showcases a revolutionary approach to digital marketing.
- **Educational Influencer and Analytics Guide:** Active in academia, sharing expertise as a Marketing Advisory Board member and Analytics mentor at Seattle University, guiding upcoming professionals.
- **Leader and Revenue Generator:** Led major projects, blending tech and business to drive innovation and impressive results, achieving over 750 million USD in revenue across various business sectors .

#AIInMarketing #RevenueMaestro #LeadershipInTech
#MachineLearningExpert #DigitalStrategyGuru
#AdvancedAnalytics #StrategicGrowthHacker #AIForRevenue

WWW.LINKEDIN.COM/IN/DINESH-KUMAR-CHINNASAMY/

THE REVENUE ENGINEER

Dmitrii Mergus

Tampa, Florida

- Position: CEO of AI Marketing Engineers
- Experience: 20+ years
- Education: M.S. in Mining and Mineral Engineering

600 million+ USD in revenue through Data Analysis:
A Journey through Mathematics to Marketing, and AI

- **Math to Marketing Mogul:** From acing international math and physics Olympiads to mastering 20+ years in SEO and Pay-per-click performance marketing and data science, Dmitrii's journey is marked by continuous excellence and innovation.
- **The Data Expert:** His enthusiasm for data analysis is reflected in his creation of groundbreaking revenue optimization dashboards using Tableau. Significantly enhanced ROAS and propelled multimillion-dollar sales.
- **AI Advocate and Educator:** Blends passion for data with a deep understanding of artificial intelligence, positioning not just as a practitioner but as a leading educator in AI Marketing.
- **Revenue Engineer:** As the brain behind multimillion-dollar campaigns for the world's largest online jewelry retailer, set multiple Revenue records and benchmarks in annual sales and ROAS. Generated over 600 million+ USD in revenue.

#MathToMarketing #AIEngineer # MarketingGuru
#GoogleAdsMaestro #PLAShoppingPro #PythonDataAnalysis
#MarketingStrategist #TableauTactician #MarketingInnovator

WWW.LINKEDIN.COM/IN/DMITRII-MERGUS/

HOLY ****!

MARKETING

FUTURE IS HERE

A **Prompt** is a sentence up to 1000 characters or less, that describes to AI WHAT you want.

Here are some examples.

> "Help me write a marketing plan"

> "Write a engaging Blog post about NY real estate market"

> "Help me plan a 10 day trip to Italy with children"

Prompts can be
very short or
very long!

"Help me write a marketing plan "

VS

Act as a seasoned marketing consultant. Your goal is to write a marketing plan (keep it short).

Step 1. Begin by inquiring about the nature and operations of my company to gain a thorough understanding of the business landscape. Only once you have a comprehensive grasp of business, transition into crafting a tailored marketing plan.

Step 2. Write a marketing plan. This plan should address the following components: Executive Summary: Start with a concise overview that encapsulates the main goals and strategies of the proposed marketing plan.
Make sure to include (Market Research, Marketing Goals, Strategies and Tactics, Budget, Measurement and Analysis, Timeline)

The final output should be a structured marketing plan ready to be refined and implemented by my company, designed to increase brand awareness, customer engagement, and sales revenue.

Let's look at some prompt elements

Act as a seasoned marketing consultant. `Set a role`

Your goal is to write a marketing plan (keep it short). `Set your goal`

Step 1. Begin by inquiring about the nature and operations of my company to gain a thorough understanding of the business landscape. Only once you have a comprehensive grasp of business, transition into crafting a tailored marketing plan. `Step 1 Context`

Step 2. Write a marketing plan. This plan should address the following components: Executive Summary: Start with a concise overview that encapsulates the main goals and strategies of the proposed marketing plan.
Make sure to include (Market Research, Marketing Goals, Strategies and Tactics, Budget, Measurement and Analysis, Timeline) `Step 2` `Clear, detailed Instructions`

The final output should be a structured marketing plan ready to be refined and implemented by my company, designed to increase brand awareness, customer engagement, and sales revenue. `Output format`

OUTPUT EXAMPLE

A Real Estate Services: Virtual Home Tours Inc.
Location: New York City, NY
What they offer: 360-degree virtual home tours for properties on sale or rent.
Target Audience: Homebuyers, renters, and real estate agents looking for a modern way to showcase properties without physical visits

Thank you for providing details about Virtual Home Tours Inc. Based on the information you've provided, here is a marketing plan tailored for your business.

Executive Summary

Virtual Home Tours Inc. leverages cutting-edge 360-degree video technology to offer immersive virtual home tours for clients in New York City. As the real estate market continues to embrace digital solutions, our marketing plan is designed to position Virtual Home Tours as the go-to service for homebuyers, renters, and real estate agents. The aim is to increase brand awareness, customer engagement, and ultimately, sales revenue through strategic marketing initiatives.

Market Research

Industry Analysis: The real estate industry is increasingly digital, with a growing number of transactions initiated or completed online. The COVID-19 pandemic has accelerated this trend, with virtual tours becoming a necessity.

Customer Insights: Our target customers are tech-savvy individuals who appreciate the convenience of online tools. Real estate agents are also looking for innovative ways to serve clients remotely.

Competitive Analysis: Competitors range from traditional real estate photographers to other virtual tour providers. Virtual Home Tours Inc. must differentiate itself by offering superior tour quality, user experience, and customer service.

Marketing Goals

1. Increase brand awareness by 30% within the next quarter.
2. Achieve a 20% rise in customer engagement through online channels.
3. Boost sales revenue by 25% over the next six months.
4. Expand to two additional cities by the end of the year.

Strategies and Tactics

Content Marketing: Create high-quality content showcasing virtual tour benefits, integrating SEO to improve search visibility.

Social Media Campaigns: Utilize platforms like Instagram, LinkedIn, and Facebook to reach both homebuyers/renters and real estate agents.

Partnership and Collaboration: Partner with local real estate agencies to offer exclusive deals on virtual tour packages.

KEY PROMPT ELEMENTS

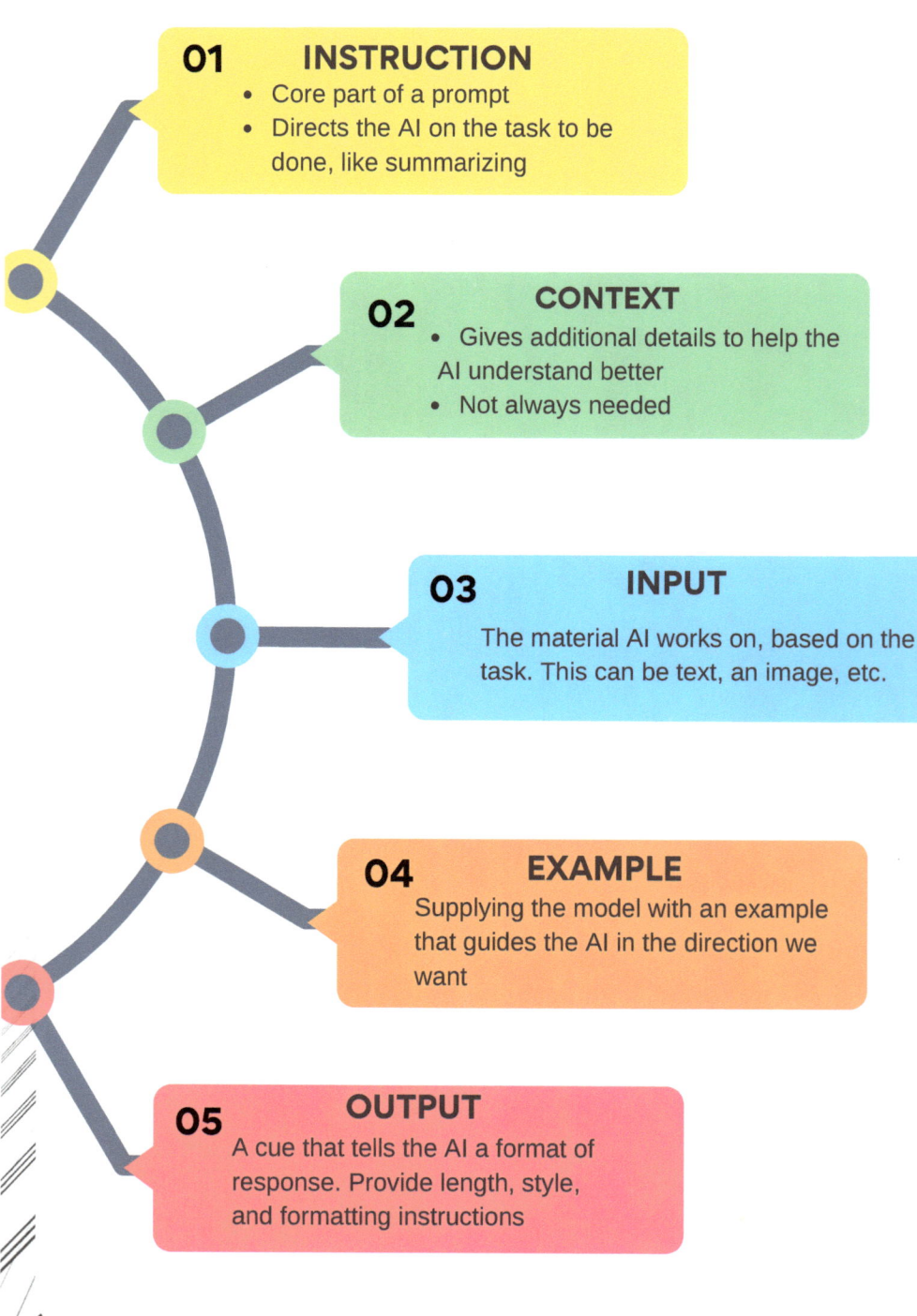

01 INSTRUCTION
- Core part of a prompt
- Directs the AI on the task to be done, like summarizing

02 CONTEXT
- Gives additional details to help the AI understand better
- Not always needed

03 INPUT
The material AI works on, based on the task. This can be text, an image, etc.

04 EXAMPLE
Supplying the model with an example that guides the AI in the direction we want

05 OUTPUT
A cue that tells the AI a format of response. Provide length, style, and formatting instructions

AI MARKETING ENGINEERS BEST PRACTICES

 **01** BE CLEAR AND SPECIFIC

 **02** CRAFT DETAILED PROMPTS

 **03** INCLUDE CONTEXT AND EXAMPLES

 04 EXPERIMENT WITH DIFFERENT PHRASINGS

05 ALWAYS VALIDATE RESULTS!

Prompt Types:

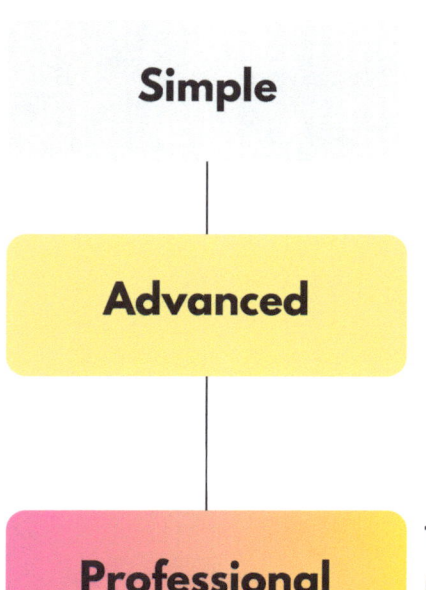

Simple

Short and simple question like "Help me write a marketing plan"

Advanced

This might include various key prompt elements such as assigning role, provide goal, context, detailed instructions in multiple steps and output format

Professional

This book doesn't cover professional prompts because they are complex and lengthy. These are up to 3-4 pages long and involve managing many parameters to guide AI creativity. They can access the internet to gather updated information and work with external tools such as Google Docs and Zapier AI actions.
GPTs and these prompts are typically used alongside APIs through frameworks like LangChain and platforms such as LLM Studio to meet specific business requirements

Here are some great **starter prompts**

① AI Content

MARKETING PROMPTS

Content is really important! It helps businesses talk to customers.

Have fun trying these ideas in ChatGPT.

1. "Provide 10 fresh **content ideas** for promoting our [your product] product"

2. "Create a detailed **content strategy plan** for the next quarter focusing on promoting our new [your product] product"

3. "Step 1. Ask me about my business and product to promote. Step 2. Help draft a **content calendar** for the next three months with a focus on our new product launches"

4. "Step 1. Ask me about my business and product to promote. Step 2. Suggest 3 **creative content formats** optimized for marketing to showcase our [product/service]"

5. "Step 1. Ask me about my business and product to promote. Step 2. Write a **compelling blog post** about the benefits of our products and business"

"COMPELLING BLOG POST" OUTPUT EXAMPLE

A Step 1. Ask me about my business and product to promote.
Step 2. Write a compelling blog post about the benefits of our products and business

Step 1: Tell me about your business and product that you'd like to promote. What does your business do, and what is unique about your product?

Step 2: Once I have more information about your business and product, I'll be happy to write a compelling blog post highlighting the benefits and unique selling points of your offerings.

A online personal trainer for Fitness enthusiasts and individuals looking for structured workout.

Great! Now that I have some information about your business, which is an online personal training service for fitness enthusiasts and individuals seeking structured workouts, let's proceed with a compelling blog post to promote your services:

Title: Unlock Your Full Fitness Potential with Our Online Personal Training

In today's fast-paced world, staying fit and healthy is more important than ever. However, finding the time, motivation, and expertise to craft a personalized fitness regimen can be a daunting task. That's where we come in – your dedicated online personal trainers, ready to transform your fitness journey into an exhilarating and results-driven experience.

The Benefits of Our Online Personal Training:

1. Personalization for Optimal Results

One-size-fits-all workouts simply don't cut it. Our online personal trainers understand that every individual has unique goals, body types, and fitness levels. That's why we create tailored workout plans designed specifically for you. Whether you're aiming for weight loss, muscle gain, improved endurance, or all of the above, we've got you covered.

2. Flexibility to Fit Your Life

Life can be unpredictable, but your fitness routine doesn't have to be. With our online training, you decide when and where you work out. Whether you're an early bird, a night owl, or somewhere in between, we'll adapt to your schedule. All you need is an internet connection, and you're ready to train.

3. Expert Guidance at Your Fingertips

Our team of certified fitness trainers brings years of experience and expertise to the table. Through our online platform, you'll have direct access to your personal trainer, allowing you

② AI Social Media
MARKETING PROMPTS

Social media is great!
It helps people learn about your business.

Enjoy trying out these ideas in ChatGPT or other LLMs.

1. "Suggest a list of 20 relevant **hashtags** for our [your product] product"

2. "Create compelling **ad copy** for our Facebook and Instagram ads promoting the [product/service]"

3. "Step 1: Research the latest trends in social media marketing for the [industry]. Step 2: Write engaging **social media posts** considering trends"

4. "Suggest creative ways to **increase engagement** on Instagram account for [product/service]"

5. "Step 1. Ask me about my business and product to promote. Step 2. Find marketing personas for my business Step 3. Suggest the **best times and days to post** on our social media channels to maximize engagement"

"TIME TO POST" OUTPUT EXAMPLE

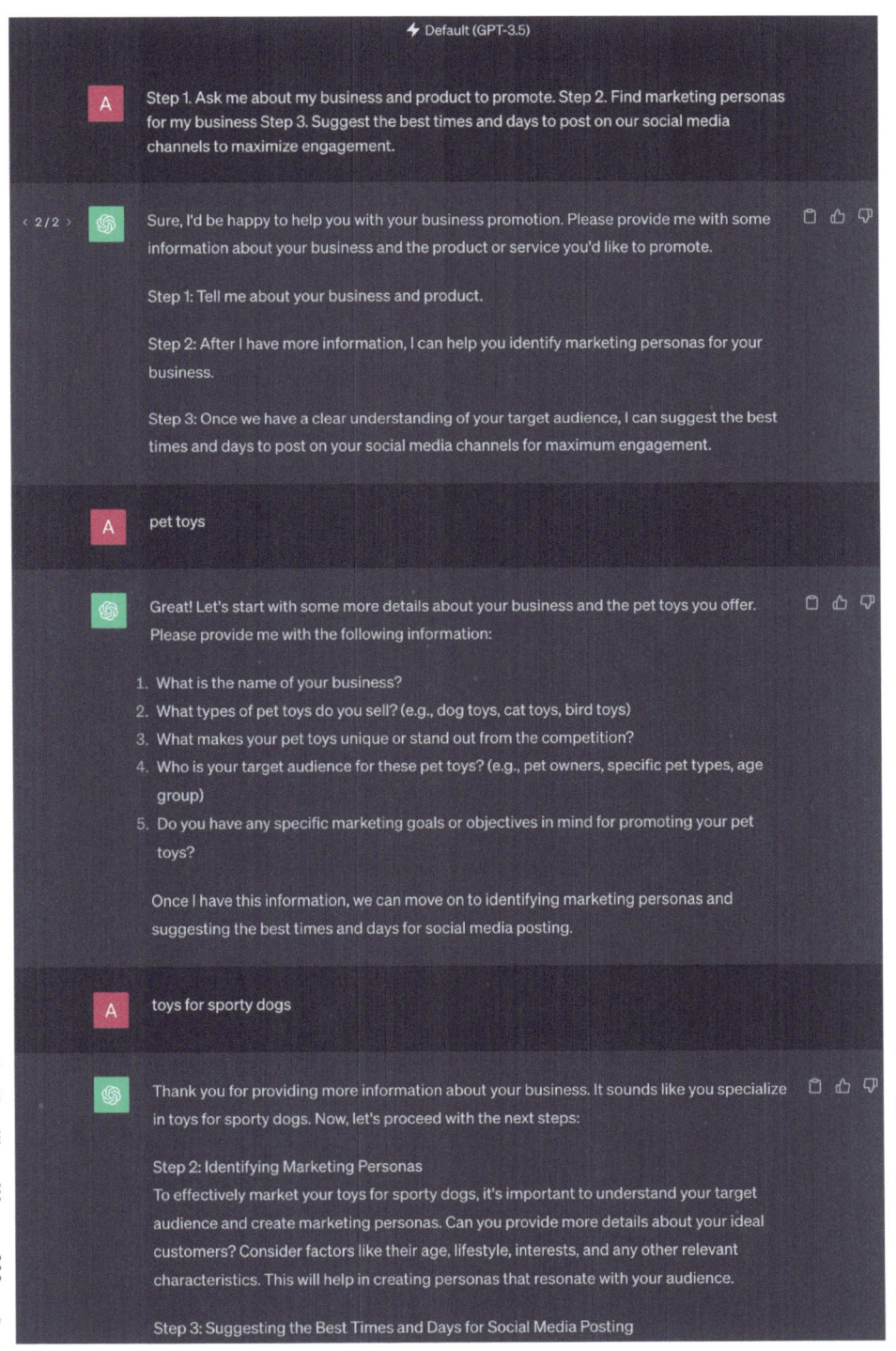

⚡ Default (GPT-3.5)

A Step 1. Ask me about my business and product to promote. Step 2. Find marketing personas for my business Step 3. Suggest the best times and days to post on our social media channels to maximize engagement.

‹ 2 / 2 › Sure, I'd be happy to help you with your business promotion. Please provide me with some information about your business and the product or service you'd like to promote.

Step 1: Tell me about your business and product.

Step 2: After I have more information, I can help you identify marketing personas for your business.

Step 3: Once we have a clear understanding of your target audience, I can suggest the best times and days to post on your social media channels for maximum engagement.

A pet toys

Great! Let's start with some more details about your business and the pet toys you offer. Please provide me with the following information:

1. What is the name of your business?
2. What types of pet toys do you sell? (e.g., dog toys, cat toys, bird toys)
3. What makes your pet toys unique or stand out from the competition?
4. Who is your target audience for these pet toys? (e.g., pet owners, specific pet types, age group)
5. Do you have any specific marketing goals or objectives in mind for promoting your pet toys?

Once I have this information, we can move on to identifying marketing personas and suggesting the best times and days for social media posting.

A toys for sporty dogs

Thank you for providing more information about your business. It sounds like you specialize in toys for sporty dogs. Now, let's proceed with the next steps:

Step 2: Identifying Marketing Personas
To effectively market your toys for sporty dogs, it's important to understand your target audience and create marketing personas. Can you provide more details about your ideal customers? Consider factors like their age, lifestyle, interests, and any other relevant characteristics. This will help in creating personas that resonate with your audience.

Step 3: Suggesting the Best Times and Days for Social Media Posting

③ AI Search Engine Optimization

MARKETING PROMPTS

SEO is crucial for people to find your business online.

Invest in SEO if you don't want to pay for your traffic

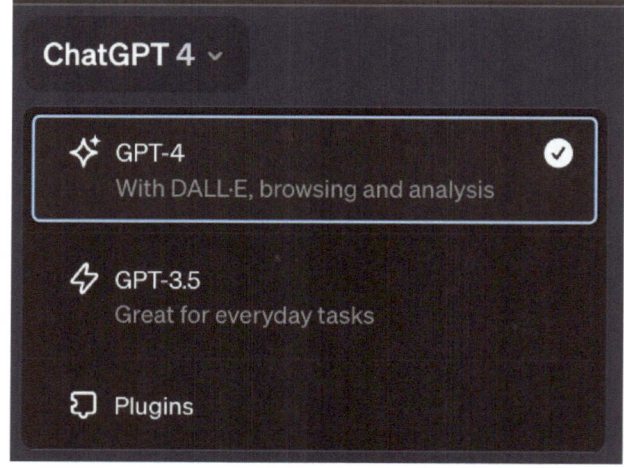

1. "Step 1: Conduct a web search to identify the latest **SEO best practices** for this year. Step 2: Analyze my website [yourwebsite.com] and provide suggestions to improve its SEO based on the identified best practices"

2. "Step 1. Find top 5 keywords related to [my business] and show their monthly search volume as table Step 2. provide 3 SEO title ideas incorporating the keywords with high keyword density Step 3. write **SEO optimized blog post** using LSI and NLP keywords"

3. "List best practices for optimizing **landing pages** on websites for SEO"

4. "Act as a SEO specialist and create a **6-month SEO plan** focusing on improving organic rankings and traffic"

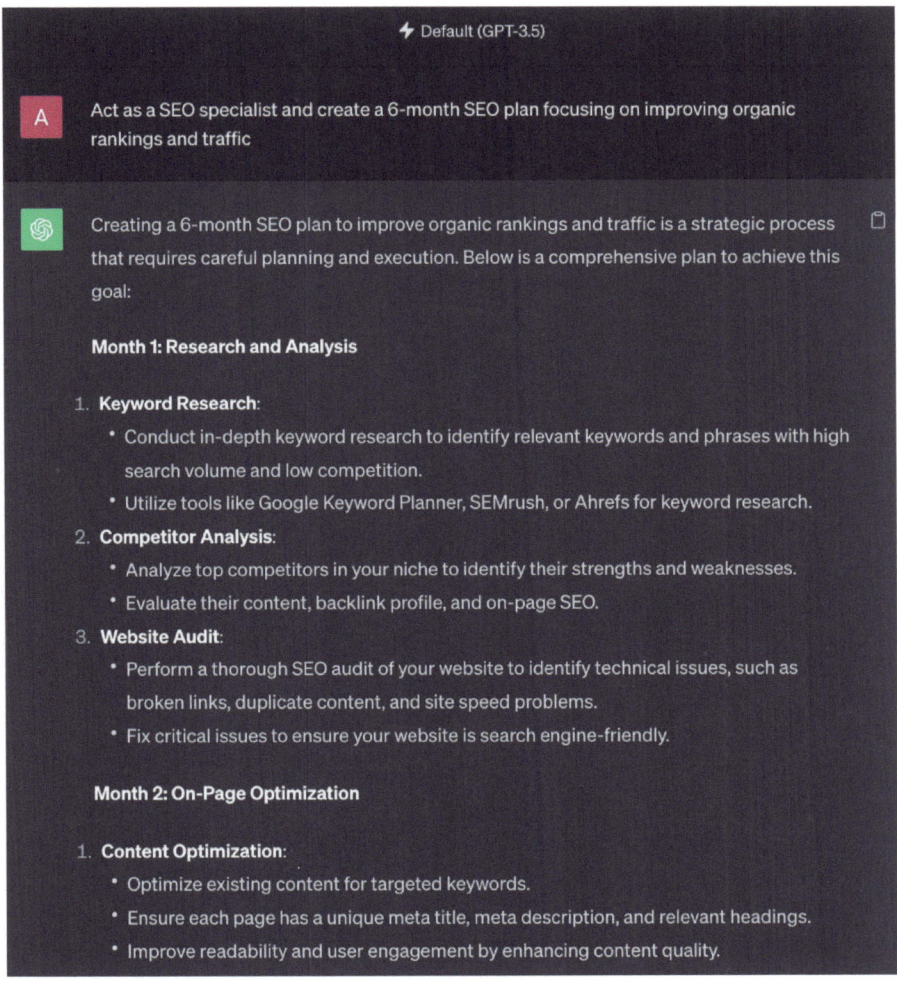

⚡ Default (GPT-3.5)

A Act as a SEO specialist and create a 6-month SEO plan focusing on improving organic rankings and traffic

Creating a 6-month SEO plan to improve organic rankings and traffic is a strategic process that requires careful planning and execution. Below is a comprehensive plan to achieve this goal:

Month 1: Research and Analysis

1. **Keyword Research**:
   * Conduct in-depth keyword research to identify relevant keywords and phrases with high search volume and low competition.
   * Utilize tools like Google Keyword Planner, SEMrush, or Ahrefs for keyword research.
2. **Competitor Analysis**:
   * Analyze top competitors in your niche to identify their strengths and weaknesses.
   * Evaluate their content, backlink profile, and on-page SEO.
3. **Website Audit**:
   * Perform a thorough SEO audit of your website to identify technical issues, such as broken links, duplicate content, and site speed problems.
   * Fix critical issues to ensure your website is search engine-friendly.

Month 2: On-Page Optimization

1. **Content Optimization**:
   * Optimize existing content for targeted keywords.
   * Ensure each page has a unique meta title, meta description, and relevant headings.
   * Improve readability and user engagement by enhancing content quality.

5. "Provide a checklist for optimizing our website for **local SEO**, focusing on [your location] and [your industry]"

"LOCAL SEO" OUTPUT EXAMPLE

Provide a checklist for optimizing our website for local SEO, focusing on Atlanta, GA and [roofing] industry

Optimizing your website for local SEO in the roofing industry in Atlanta, GA requires a strategic approach. Here's a checklist to help you get started:

1. **Keyword Research:**
   - Identify relevant keywords for your business, such as "roofing services Atlanta," "Atlanta roofing contractors," and specific long-tail keywords like "emergency roof repair in Atlanta."
2. **Google My Business (GMB) Optimization:**
   - Claim and verify your Google My Business listing.
   - Ensure your business name, address, and phone number (NAP) are consistent across all online platforms.
   - Select the most relevant categories for your business.
   - Add high-quality images of your roofing work.
   - Encourage customer reviews and respond to them promptly.
3. **On-Page SEO:**
   - Optimize meta titles and descriptions with local keywords.
   - Include Atlanta-related keywords in your content.
   - Create high-quality, informative, and locally relevant content.
   - Use header tags (H1, H2, H3) to structure your content.
   - Add schema markup to provide search engines with structured data about your business.
4. **Mobile Optimization:**
   - Ensure your website is mobile-friendly and loads quickly on mobile devices.
   - Use responsive design for a seamless mobile experience.
5. **Local Citations:**
   - Create consistent citations on local business directories like Yelp, YellowPages, and Angie's List.
   - Include accurate NAP information in these citations.
6. **Link Building:**
   - Build high-quality, relevant backlinks from local websites, directories, and industry-related sources.
   - Guest post on local blogs or industry websites.
7. **Local Content Marketing:**
   - Create and promote content that is specific to Atlanta and the roofing industry.
   - Participate in local events or sponsor local organizations and get coverage on your website.

MARKETING PROMPTS

YouTube is the second largest search engine and has a big influence.

Podcasts are enjoyable and easy to access, making them the quickest-growing type of media right now.

ON AIR

1. "Provide 10 creative **content ideas** for our YouTube channel focusing on [your industry/product]"

2. "Draft a compelling **script for a product** explainer video for our new [product name]"

3. "Step 1. Ask me about my business and product to promote. Step 2. Suggest 5 **best ideas** for engaging live streaming content on platforms like Facebook and YouTube"

4. "Step 1: Identify and list 10 potential guests who are experts in [your industry or topic]. Step 2: Draft personalized **outreach emails** inviting them to be guests on our podcast"

GPT4 PROMPT

5. "Step 1: Research trending topics in [your industry or topic]. Step 2: **Plan the next 5 episodes** of the podcast around these trending topics"

"PLAN THE NEXT 5 EPISODES" OUTPUT EXAMPLE

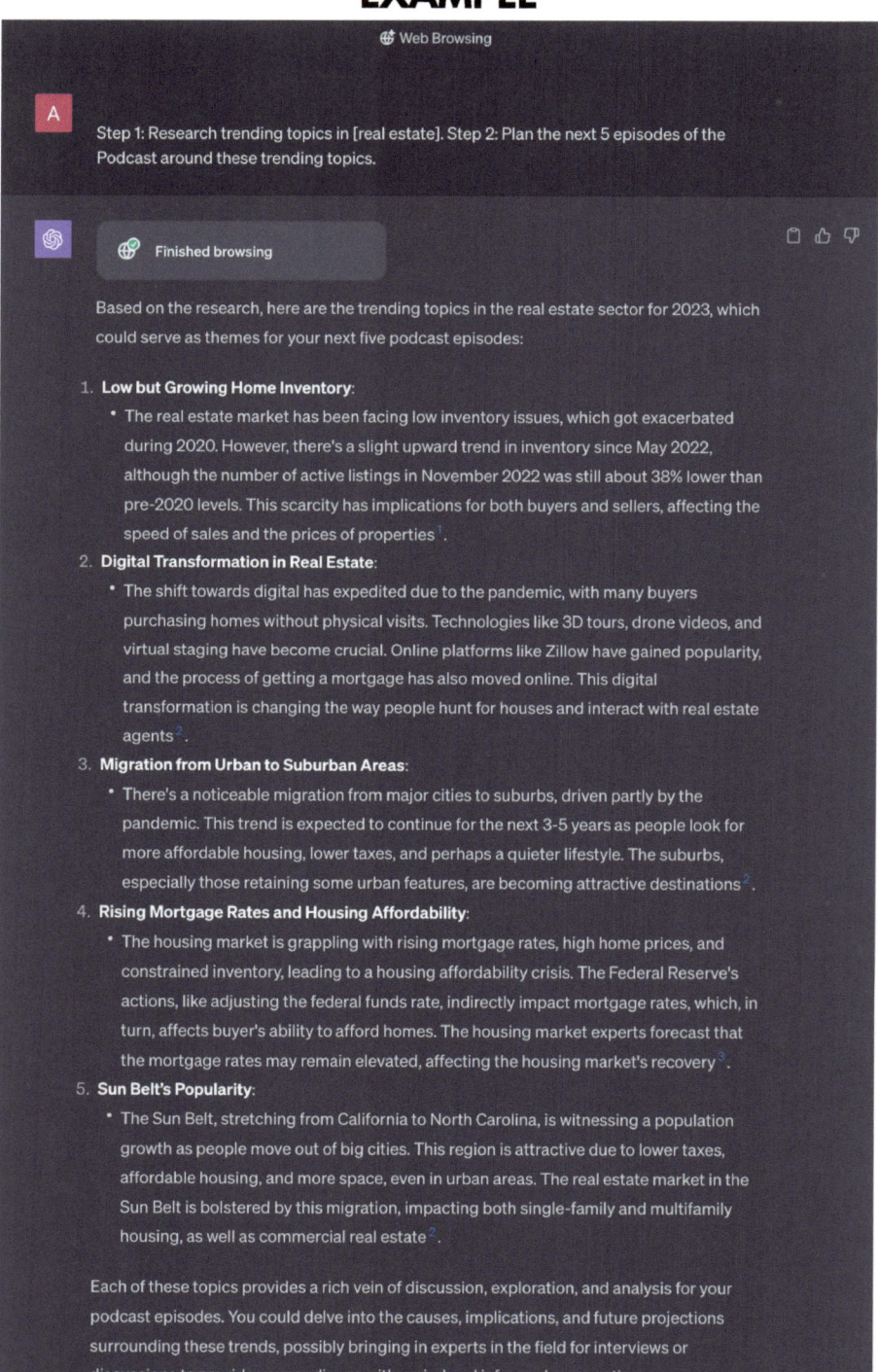

🌐 Web Browsing

A

Step 1: Research trending topics in [real estate]. Step 2: Plan the next 5 episodes of the Podcast around these trending topics.

🌐 Finished browsing

Based on the research, here are the trending topics in the real estate sector for 2023, which could serve as themes for your next five podcast episodes:

1. **Low but Growing Home Inventory**:
   - The real estate market has been facing low inventory issues, which got exacerbated during 2020. However, there's a slight upward trend in inventory since May 2022, although the number of active listings in November 2022 was still about 38% lower than pre-2020 levels. This scarcity has implications for both buyers and sellers, affecting the speed of sales and the prices of properties [1].
2. **Digital Transformation in Real Estate**:
   - The shift towards digital has expedited due to the pandemic, with many buyers purchasing homes without physical visits. Technologies like 3D tours, drone videos, and virtual staging have become crucial. Online platforms like Zillow have gained popularity, and the process of getting a mortgage has also moved online. This digital transformation is changing the way people hunt for houses and interact with real estate agents [2].
3. **Migration from Urban to Suburban Areas**:
   - There's a noticeable migration from major cities to suburbs, driven partly by the pandemic. This trend is expected to continue for the next 3-5 years as people look for more affordable housing, lower taxes, and perhaps a quieter lifestyle. The suburbs, especially those retaining some urban features, are becoming attractive destinations [2].
4. **Rising Mortgage Rates and Housing Affordability**:
   - The housing market is grappling with rising mortgage rates, high home prices, and constrained inventory, leading to a housing affordability crisis. The Federal Reserve's actions, like adjusting the federal funds rate, indirectly impact mortgage rates, which, in turn, affects buyer's ability to afford homes. The housing market experts forecast that the mortgage rates may remain elevated, affecting the housing market's recovery [3].
5. **Sun Belt's Popularity**:
   - The Sun Belt, stretching from California to North Carolina, is witnessing a population growth as people move out of big cities. This region is attractive due to lower taxes, affordable housing, and more space, even in urban areas. The real estate market in the Sun Belt is bolstered by this migration, impacting both single-family and multifamily housing, as well as commercial real estate [2].

Each of these topics provides a rich vein of discussion, exploration, and analysis for your podcast episodes. You could delve into the causes, implications, and future projections surrounding these trends, possibly bringing in experts in the field for interviews or discussions to provide your audience with varied and informed perspectives.

MARKETING PROMPTS

Email marketing can be a cost-effective way to reach your target audience directly with personalized content.

It helps you build a relationship with your audience while driving traffic to your website.

1. "Step 1: Research effective **email list building strategies**. Step 2: Propose a plan for growing our email list over the next [X] months"

2. "Write compelling **email copy** for our upcoming [event/sale/promotion], focusing on [specific benefit or feature]"

3. "Generate 10 creative **email campaign ideas** to promote our [new product/service]"

4. "Design an **A/B testing plan** to optimize the subject lines and content of our emails for better engagement."

5. "Step 1. Ask me about my business and product to promote. Step 2: Outline the stages of a well-structured **email funnel** for converting leads into customers for our product and draft engaging email content for each stage of the funnel, ensuring it aligns with the goals of that stage, provide timing for each email, like "Day 1""

"EMAIL FUNNEL" OUTPUT EXAMPLE

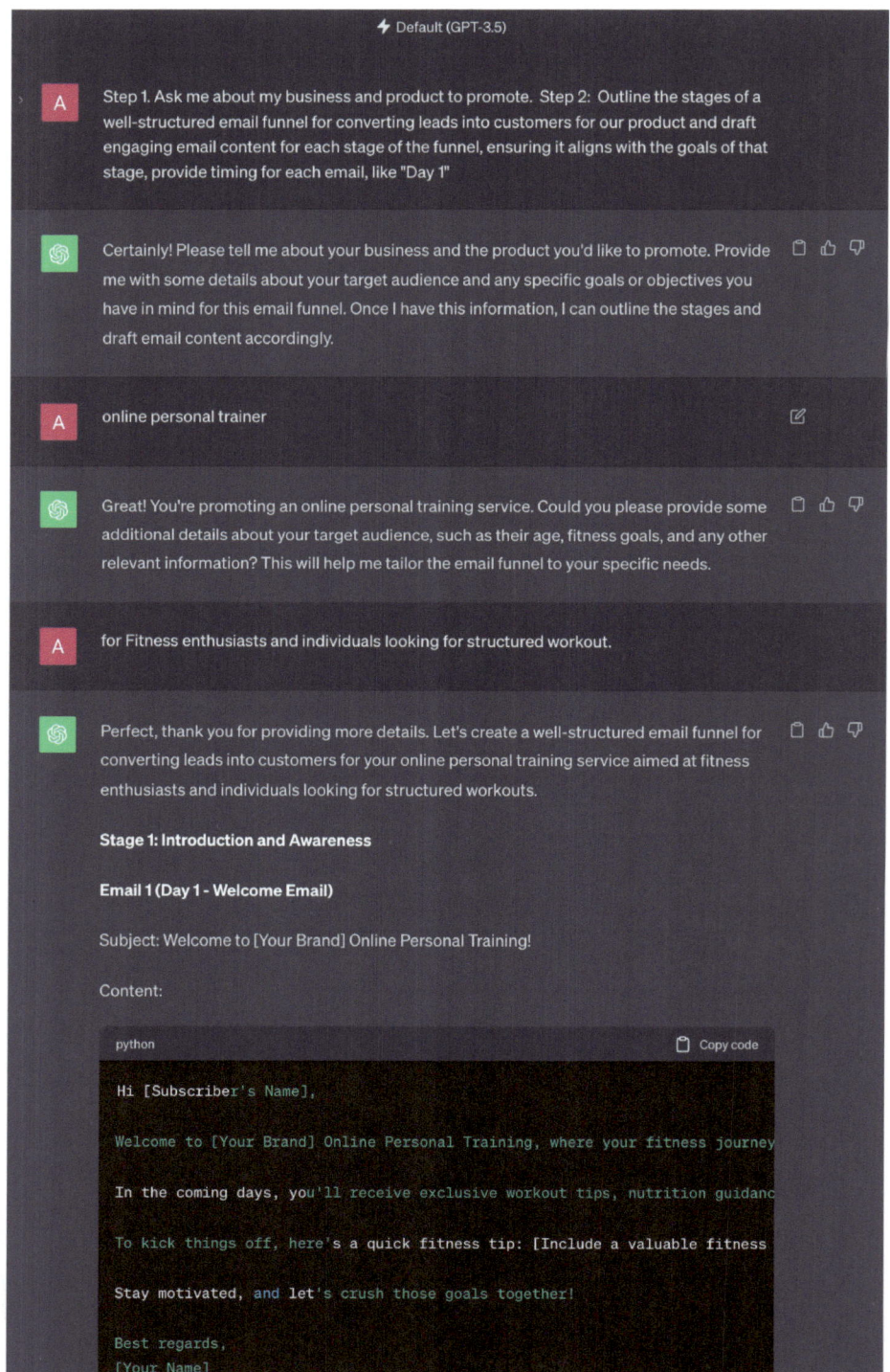

A Step 1. Ask me about my business and product to promote. Step 2: Outline the stages of a well-structured email funnel for converting leads into customers for our product and draft engaging email content for each stage of the funnel, ensuring it aligns with the goals of that stage, provide timing for each email, like "Day 1"

Certainly! Please tell me about your business and the product you'd like to promote. Provide me with some details about your target audience and any specific goals or objectives you have in mind for this email funnel. Once I have this information, I can outline the stages and draft email content accordingly.

A online personal trainer

Great! You're promoting an online personal training service. Could you please provide some additional details about your target audience, such as their age, fitness goals, and any other relevant information? This will help me tailor the email funnel to your specific needs.

A for Fitness enthusiasts and individuals looking for structured workout.

Perfect, thank you for providing more details. Let's create a well-structured email funnel for converting leads into customers for your online personal training service aimed at fitness enthusiasts and individuals looking for structured workouts.

Stage 1: Introduction and Awareness

Email 1 (Day 1 - Welcome Email)

Subject: Welcome to [Your Brand] Online Personal Training!

Content:

```python
Hi [Subscriber's Name],

Welcome to [Your Brand] Online Personal Training, where your fitness journey

In the coming days, you'll receive exclusive workout tips, nutrition guidanc

To kick things off, here's a quick fitness tip: [Include a valuable fitness

Stay motivated, and let's crush those goals together!

Best regards,
[Your Name]
```

Stage 2: Education and Engagement

Email 2 (Day 3 - Educational Content)

Subject: The Science of Effective Workouts

Content:

```python
Hello [Subscriber's Name],

Understanding the science behind effective workouts is essential to achievin

[Provide educational content about workout principles, such as progressive o

Ready to put this knowledge into action? Stay tuned for your personalized wo

Stay committed,
[Your Name]
```

Stage 3: Personalization and Offer

Email 3 (Day 7 - Personalized Workout Plan)

Subject: Your Customized Workout Plan Awaits!

Content:

```vbnet
Hi [Subscriber's Name],

We're excited to present your personalized workout plan tailored to help you

- [List key features of the workout plan, e.g., duration, exercises, intensi
- [Mention any tracking tools or apps you provide]
- [Include an exclusive offer for the first month or a free trial]

Ready to get started? Click below to access your workout plan and start your

[Button: Access My Plan]

Remember, we're here to support you every step of the way. If you have any o

To your success!
[Your Name]
```

Stage 4: Follow-up and Encouragement

Email 4 (Day 14 - Check-in)

Subject: How's Your Fitness Journey Going?

Be aware of AI Detection

AI detection Tools

AI detection tools helps to figure out text quality and relevance if a piece of text was written by a computer or a human. These tools often use various methods to analyze text patterns, which typically indicate machine-generated content.

Your Text is AI/GPT Generated

97.04%
AI GPT*

Tool	Pros	Cons	URL
Winston AI	Good accuracy, highlights AI text, Free 7 day, 2,000 word scan trial	Costs $19/month, sign-up required	https://gowinston.ai/
Originality. AI	Good accuracy, detects GPT-4 and paraphrasing tools	Costs at least $14.95, sign-up required	https://originality.ai/
Sapling	Free, no false positives, no sign-up required	Unclear highlighting	https://sapling.ai/ai-content-detector
CopyLeaks	Free, no sign-up required	limit on daily checks	https://copyleaks.com/ai-content-detector
ZeroGPT	Free, gives percentage and highlights, no sign-up required	character limits on free version	https://www.zerogpt.com/

Google Guidance on AI Content

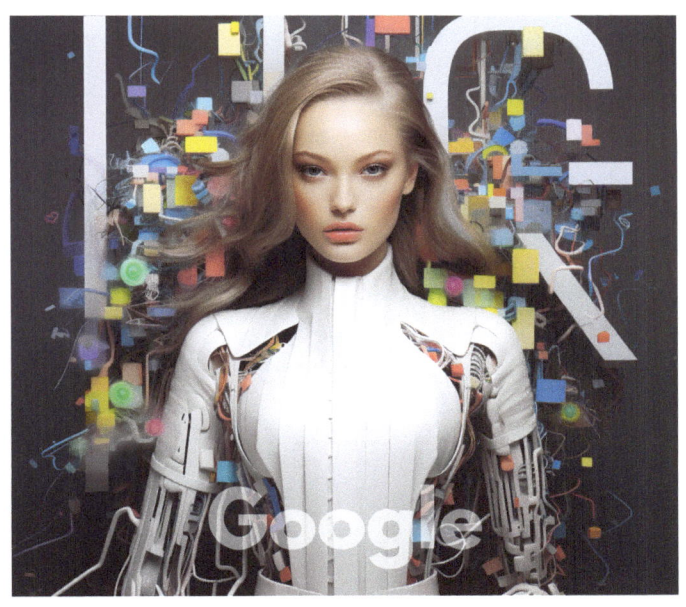

Google prioritizes high-quality content, regardless of whether it's generated by humans or AI,

and advises publishers to produce helpful, people-first content that demonstrates expertise, experience, authoritativeness, and trustworthiness (E-E-A-T)

AI Art

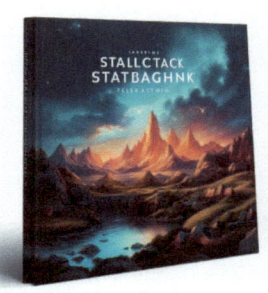

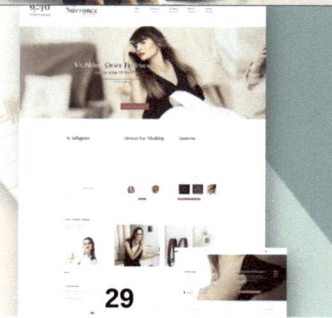

MARKETING PROMPTS

1. "**Create a logo** for a [specific type of business e.g., ' real estate'] named [specific name e.g., 'EXO']"

2. "Create a winning **landing page design** for [specific topic e.g., 'auto loan website']"

MARKETING PROMPTS

3.

> "Design a [style e.g., 'modern'] **advertisement poster** for [your industry e.g., 'Seattle Real Estate']"

4.

> "Design a **cover for an eBook** titled [title e.g., 'When to buy a house'] covering [provide details e.g., 'real estate topics']"

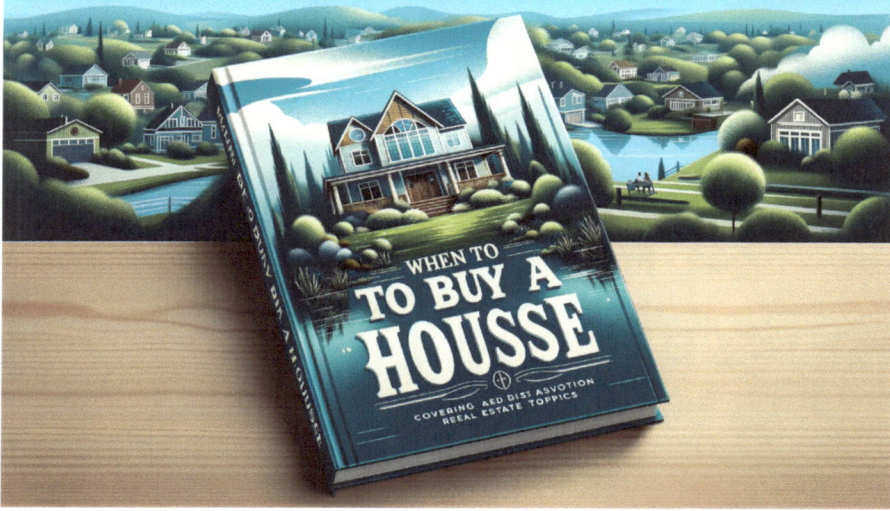

MARKETING PROMPTS

5. "Create a **business card** using the following details [details]"

6. "Design a [style] **advertisement poster** for [your industry]"

MARKETING PROMPTS

7. "**Design packaging** for our [product e.g., 'diamond engagement rings']"

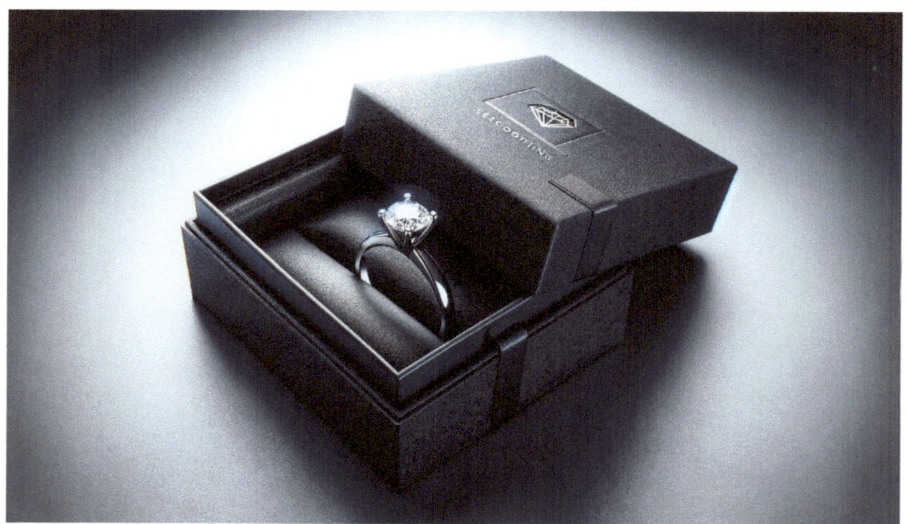

8. "Design [style e.g.,'cat'] **icon pack** for [website e.g., 'pet store']"

MARKETING PROMPTS

9. "**Design an illustration** showcasing [details e.g., 'women's designer clothes']"

10. "Design a **viral youtube thumbnail** that grabs attention and showcases [details, e.g., 'Real Estate Trends']"

TOP AI TOOLS

CHATBOTS

ChatGPT Claude Bard/Gemini Perplexity Bing

CONTENT GENERATION

Jasper Notion Writer Frase

IMAGE GENERATION

Writer Adobe Firefly Stable Diffusion DALL·E 3 Bing Image Create

AUDIO

Descript Adobe podcast Murf Otter

VIDEO

Runway Fliki Opus Clip Synthesia Filmora

OTHER

Grammarly Quilbot Tome Tome Meshcapade

Motion Aomni Mem Zapier AI Actions

ChatGPT on Mobile

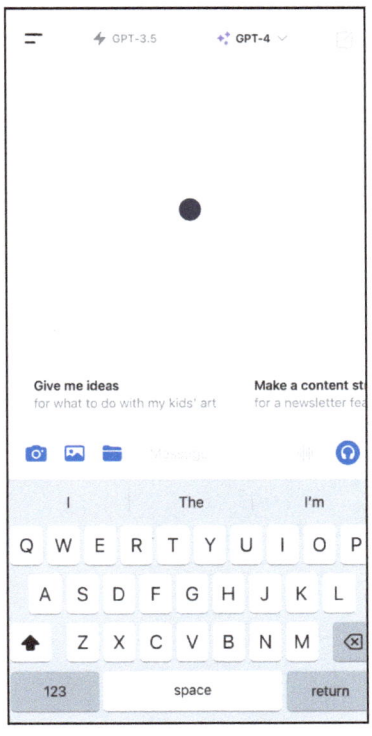

ChatGPT Mobile App:

You can use GPT on mobile devices using the following methods:

You can use ChatGPT on mobile devices via the browser (e.g. Google Chrome) or via the **official ChatGPT app for iOS** or Android. ChatGPT is free to use and download.

ChatGPT Finds Voice:

OpenAI has enabled ChatGPT with the ability to engage in verbal conversations, making your interactions more personal and accessible than ever. We experienced improved prompting and outputs through the conversational nature of ChatGPT.

ChatGPT Vision

ChatGPT Vision:

ChatGPT can now understand and respond to visual inputs. Whether it's analyzing graphs, and images or generating artwork, the AI adapts to your visual prompts seamlessly. e.g.) take a picture of your fridge and ask ChatGPT to suggest a recipe or take a picture and ask a question.

Create your own GPT: (ChatGPT Plus Users)

Creating a GPT means making a custom version of ChatGPT that you can set up to do specific tasks or answer questions about certain topics. It's like building your own chatbot that knows exactly what you need.

Below are some default options of GPT provided by OpenAI

My GPTs

Create a GPT Beta
Customize a version of ChatGPT for a specific purpose

Made by OpenAI

DALL·E
Let me turn your imagination into imagery

Data Analysis
Drop in any files and I can help analyze and visualize your data

ChatGPT Classic
The latest version of GPT-4 with no additional capabilities

Game Time
I can quickly explain board games or card games to players of any age. Let the games begin!

The Negotiator
I'll help you advocate for yourself and get better outcomes. Become a great negotiator.

Customize GPTs

Creative Writing Coach
I'm eager to read your work and give you feedback to improve your skills.

Cosmic Dream
Visionary painter of digital wonder

Tech Support Advisor
From setting up a printer to troubleshooting a device, I'm here to help you step-by-step.

Coloring Book Hero
Take any idea and turn it into whimsical coloring book pages

Laundry Buddy
Ask me anything about stains, settings, sorting and everything laundry.

Sous Chef
I'll give you recipes based on the foods you love and ingredients you have.

Sticker Whiz
I'll help turn your wildest dreams into die-cut stickers, shipped right to your door.

Math Mentor
I help parents help their kids with math. Need a 9pm refresher on geometry proofs? I'm here for you.

Hot Mods
Let's modify your image into something really wild. Upload an image and let's go!

Mocktail Mixologist
I'll make any party a blast with mocktail recipes with whatever ingredients you have on hand.

genz 4 meme
i help u understand the lingo & the latest memes

The Journey of a Business Prompt Engineer

1. **UNDERSTAND THE NEED FOR AI IN BUSINESS**

2. **UNDERSTAND LLM LIMITATIONS**

3. **EXPLORE OTHER AI TOOLS**

4. **EXPLORE PLUGINS AND AI AUTOMATION**

5. **LEARN PROMPT ENGINEERING**

6. **VALIDATE RESULTS**

7. **ITERATIVE DEVELOPMENT**

8. **CONTINUOUS LEARNING AND IMPROVEMENT**

Stay Ahead: Continuous Learning in AI Marketing

Join Our YouTube Community: AI Marketing Engineers

We're thrilled to invite you to join our vibrant YouTube community at AI Marketing Engineers! Here's why you should subscribe:

- **Expert Insights:** Learn from our team who've generated over $1 billion in the US.
- **Exclusive Content**: Access a wealth of knowledge with our free AI Marketing videos , offering top free premium AI marketing content.
- **Practical Strategies**: Discover actionable AI-driven marketing techniques.
- **Real Results:** We focus on ROI-driven approaches and provide tools and techniques that improve customer engagement, targeting, and personalization.

Marketing Engineers

@marketingengineers · 10.1K subscribers

Welcome to AI Marketing Engineers, your ⌐

aimarketingengineers.com

Time to Apply AI for Business

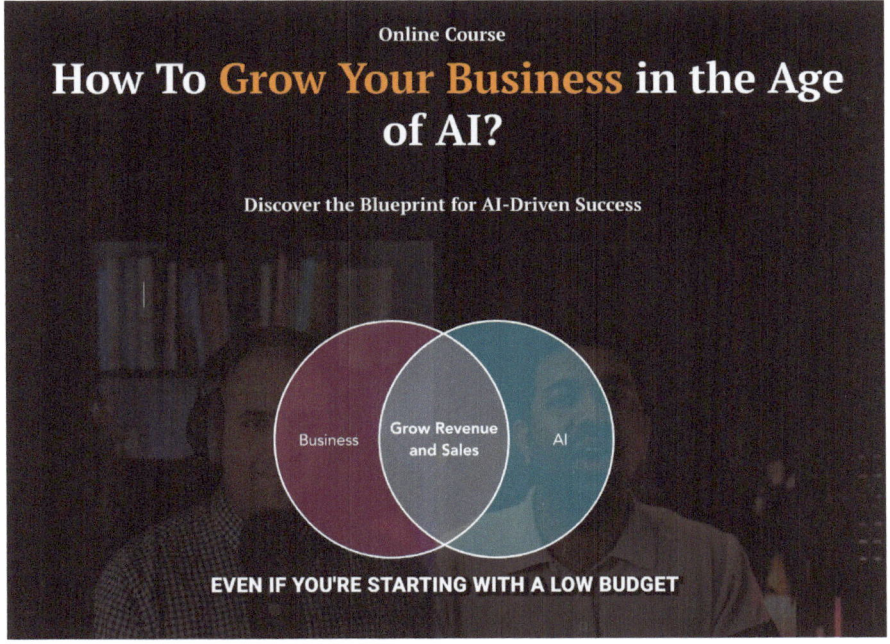

Online Course

How To Grow Your Business in the Age of AI?

Discover the Blueprint for AI-Driven Success

Business | Grow Revenue and Sales | AI

EVEN IF YOU'RE STARTING WITH A LOW BUDGET

Ready to supercharge your business with AI?

🐎 Welcome to the ultimate AI course for entrepreneurs, business owners, and tech enthusiasts!

⬛ Dive deep into ChatGPT and **prompt engineering** techniques.

⬛ You want to **boost productivity like never before** by achieving twice the output

⬛ You desire to **slash your expenses** up to 50%, all while accomplishing tasks in just half the time

AIMARKETINGENGINEERS.COM

www.ingramcontent.com/pod-product-compliance
Lightning Source LLC
Chambersburg PA
CBHW050847290526
45792CB00002B/553